The JEFFERSONIAN REPUBLICANS:

The Louisiana Purchase and the War of 1812

1800–1823

The JEFFERSONIAN REPUBLIANS:

The Louisiana Purchase and the War of 1812

1800–1823

Christopher Collier
James Lincoln Collier

BENCHMARK BOOKS

MARSHALL CAVENDISH
NEW YORK

ACKNOWLEDGMENT: The authors wish to thank Stanley Katz, Professor of Public and International Affairs, The Woodrow Wilson School, Princeton University, and David Usner, Jr., Professor of History, Cornell University, for their careful reading of the text of this volume of The Drama of American History and their thoughtful and useful comments. This work has been much improved by their notes. The authors are deeply in their debt but, of course, assume full responsibility for the substance of the work, including any errors that may appear.

Photo research by James Lincoln Collier.
COVER PHOTO: © Joslyn Art Museum
PICTURE CREDITS: The photographs in this book are used by permission and through the courtesy of : *Independence National Historic Park*: 10, 36, 60, 73. *Colonial Williamsburg Foundation*: 15. *Abby Aldrich Rockafeller Folk Art Center*: 16. *Corbis-Bettmann*: 19 (top), 19 (bottom), 28, 46, 52, 63. *Joslyn Art Museum*: 21, 23, 24, 39 (top), 39 (bottom), 40, 41, 47. *Smithsonian Institute*: 33, 65. *Prints and Photography Division, Library of Congress*: 42, 43, 50, 55 (top), 55(bottom), 66, 67, 71, 74, 76, 77, 79, 82 (top), 82 (bottom).

Benchmark Books
Marshall Cavendish Corporation
99 White Plains Road
Tarrytown, New York 10591-9001

©1999 Christopher Collier and James Lincoln Collier

Library of Congress Cataloging-in-Publication Data

Collier, Christopher, date
The Jeffersonian Republicans, 1800–1823 / Christopher Collier, James Lincoln Collier.
p. cm.   —(Drama of American history)
Includes bibliographical references (p.) and index.
Summary: Discusses the events and personalities that shaped this country, from the hotly contested election of 1800 that brought Thomas Jefferson into office through the westward expansion to the War of 1812 and James Madison's presidency.
ISBN 0-7614-0778-2 (lib. bdg.)
1. United States—Politics and government—1801–1815—Juvenile literature. 2. United States—Politics and government—1815–1861—Juvenile literature. 3. Republican Party (U.S.: 1792–1828)—History—Juvenile literature.
[1. United States—History—1801–1809. 2. United States—History—1809–1817.]
I. Collier, James Lincoln, date. II. Title. III. Series: Collier, Christopher, date Drama of American history.
                              E338.C844 1999
973.4'6–dc21   97-35909
                                                    CIP
                                                    AC

Printed in Italy

1 3 5 6 4 2

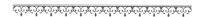

CONTENTS

PREFACE

Over many years of both teaching and writing for students at all levels, from grammar school to graduate school, it has been borne in on us that many, if not most, American history textbooks suffer from trying to include everything of any moment in the history of the nation. Students become lost in a swamp of factual information, and as a consequence lose track of how those facts fit together and why they are significant and relevant to the world today.

In this series, our effort has been to strip the vast amount of available detail down to a central core. Our aim is to draw in bold strokes, providing enough information, but no more than is necessary, to bring out the basic themes of the American story, and what they mean to us now. We believe that it is surely more important for students to grasp the underlying concepts and ideas that emerge from the movement of history, than to memorize an array of facts and figures.

The difference between this series and many standard texts lies in what has been left out. We are convinced that students will better remember the important themes if they are not buried under a heap of names, dates, and places.

In this sense, our primary goal is what might be called citizenship education. We think it is critically important for America as a nation and Americans as individuals to understand the origins and workings of the public institutions that are central to American society. We have asked ourselves again and again what is most important for citizens of our democracy to know so they can most effectively make the system work for them and the nation. For this reason, we have focused on political and institutional history, leaving social and cultural history less well developed.

This series is divided into volumes that move chronologically through the American story. Each is built around a single topic, such as the Pilgrims, the Constitutional Convention, or immigration. Each volume has been written so that it can stand alone, for students who wish to research a given topic. As a consequence, in many cases material from previous volumes is repeated, usually in abbreviated form, to set the topic in its historical context. That is to say, students of the Constitutional Convention must be given some idea of relations with England, and why the Revolution was fought, even though the material was covered in detail in a previous volume. Readers should find that each volume tells an entire story that can be read with or without reference to other volumes.

Despite our belief that it is of the first importance to outline sharply basic concepts and generalizations, we have not neglected the great dramas of American history. The stories that will hold the attention of students are here, and we believe they will help the concepts they illustrate to stick in their minds. We think, for example, that knowing of Abraham Baldwin's brave and dramatic decision to vote with the small states at the Constitutional Convention will bring alive the Connecticut Compromise, out of which grew the American Senate.

Each of these volumes has been read by esteemed specialists in its particular topic; we have benefited from their comments.

CHAPTER I

A Contested Election

The period of American history from 1800, when Thomas Jefferson was elected president, to 1817, when James Madison left office, was a momentous one. There occurred during this period at least three major events which were to shape in dramatic ways the America we are living in now.

For one, the election of 1800, which pitted Jefferson against John Adams, was the first hard-fought one in which two factions with very different ideas of what the U.S. government should do struggled for power. George Washington had been selected automatically without opposition in the first two presidential elections, and his vice president, John Adams, had succeeded him without much of a fight. But the 1800 campaign was one of the most vicious in American history. The question was, would the men in power who had lost the election now turn over their offices to the winners, who had very different ideas about where the nation ought to go? Peaceful transfer of power had not been done often in the long history of governments.

For another, during these years the United States acquired the huge piece of land between the Mississippi River and the Rocky Mountains

One of the hardest-fought elections, with much slander spewed forth by both sides, occurred in 1800 between John Adams of the Federalists (left) and Thomas Jefferson of the Republicans (right). In a general sense, these two factions were the basis for the creation of American political parties in subsequent elections.

now known as the Louisiana Purchase. It more than doubled the size of the United States. Several European nations had long eyed this vast territory, home to tens of thousands of Indians but virtually unexplored by Europeans. If the United States had not bought this land, a lot of it might have been seized by other nations. England, from its trading posts in Canada, was claiming what are now Oregon and Washington. Spain for generations had been settling California and the Southwest. Both France and Spain had claims to the newly bought land. Had the Louisiana

Purchase not been made, it is entirely possible that Oregon, Washington, and perhaps other states like Idaho and Montana might be part of Canada. Louisiana, Arkansas, Missouri, and other places might be part of a French-speaking nation. The rest of the Southwest might be a group of Hispanic nations. And California might be divided between Mexico and Russia.

Last, the period saw the inconclusive battling between the United States and England that we call the War of 1812. The United States did not really win this war, although Americans liked to think they did; but they did not lose it, either, and the final result was to bring Americans more together than they had been. After the war of 1812 Americans began to see that they were not just Georgians, Marylanders, New Yorkers, but Americans as well. And it was now clear to them, and the rest of the world, that the United States was a going concern.

But before any of this could happen, Americans had, in 1800, to get through a difficult transition in power—what we would now call a change in the party running the government. Today we are used to seeing Republicans and Democrats take turns running the government, or even sharing power, with one party holding the White House, the other the Congress. In 1800 this transfer of power was a new experience for Americans, and in order to understand why, we need to step back a few years to the previous administrations.

When the new government was started in 1789 after the Constitution was ratified, it was taken for granted that George Washington would be elected president for as many terms as he wanted. There were no political parties then, nor anything like them, and at first there was little opposition to what Washington wanted to do, especially from other politicians like James Madison and Thomas Jefferson.

Washington had for his Secretary of the Treasury the brilliant and strong-willed Alexander Hamilton. Hamilton, Washington, and others believed that the national government ought to be strong and active in

The physical layout of a nation has important effects on its policies. This was particularly so in the early days, when there were no such things as automobiles and airplanes, and goods and people had to travel by foot, sail, or horsepower. One of the key physical features in the United States is the Appalachian Mountain chain, which runs from Maine down into Georgia. While not as formidable to cross as the Rocky Mountains, which are higher and snow-covered in the winter, the Appalachians were a real obstacle to wagons carrying goods and products. Through the two hundred years from the first settlements to the early nineteenth century, newcomers built along the coast, and then slowly worked their way inland to the foot of the Appalachians. There settlement halted.

As the best farmlands along the east coast were taken up after the Revolution, people were forced to look across the mountains for space. Here, in what is now Ohio, Kentucky, Tennessee, and states further west, was the rich bottomland of the valleys associated with the system of deep rivers, many flowing into the Ohio, which, in turn, ran into the Mississippi. Rivers were critically important, for carting a lot of goods over rugged terrain covered by thick forests was nearly impossible; heavy cargoes could only go by boat or barge.

This river system was a crucial feature of the new nation. It allowed farmers west of the Appalachians to transport their products—grain, whiskey, cured meat—back over the mountains to markets in Pennsylvania, New England, the Carolinas. It was far easier to ship them by boat west along the river system into the Mississippi, then south down the Mississippi to New Orleans, where they could be sold to brokers, who would ship them by seagoing vessels to markets in the West Indies, the coastal ports of the United States, like New York and Charlestown, or to Europe. Control of the Mississippi was thus critical to the settlement of the western lands.

doing things for the general good of the country. Hamilton, in particular, had a lot of novel ideas for organizing the finances of the United States, which would require the government to take the lead in many matters. (For a discussion of Hamilton's program see *Building a New Nation* in this series.) On top of it, Washington, Hamilton, Vice President John Adams, and others felt that the voters did not have the education, the time, or even the interest to make well-informed judgments about what the government should do. This seemed especially true in complex matters of finance and diplomacy. They believed that once the people had chosen their government, they should trust it to do right and should obey the laws it put forth.

Washington, Hamilton, and the others were quite honest in believing these things, and it is certainly true that many people believed them, as some do today: The whole question of how strong and active the federal government ought to be is still a major issue in America. But others were very disturbed by such ideas. Many people thought that the federal government ought to do as little as possible, mainly taking care of relations with other nations; they felt that the states, cities, and villages were best suited to deal with the problems at home. And needless to say, many people, including both the well-to-do and the ordinary farmers who made up the bulk of the American population were angered by the idea that they ought to accept, on faith, the plans and policies of the federal government.

Among those who strongly disagreed with Washington and Hamilton were Thomas Jefferson and James Madison, good friends and Virginians, who had not only played major roles in the politics of their state but had been major figures in national politics as well. Jefferson and Madison believed that the people basically had good judgment and that the national government should get itself involved in state and local affairs as little as possible. (In fact, as presidents, both of these men extended the power of the national government much beyond what their principles should have allowed.)

During the twelve years between Washington's first inaugural in 1789, and 1800, the country became increasingly split between these two points of view. Quickly the two factions acquired names. The Washington-Hamilton group came to be called Federalists, because they favored a strong federal government; the Jefferson-Madison group were called Republicans, because they supported the republican ideal that the government belonged to the people. (This early group of Republicans had nothing to do with the modern Republican Party.)

These two factions were not political parties in the modern sense. They did not hold conventions to nominate candidates for president, did not have national headquarters or slogans or campaign buttons. But they were parties in the sense that they were collections of people who agreed, more or less, on the same set of ideas.

The election of 1800 was fought out between the Federalist and Republican factions. It was as vicious and mudslinging a campaign as we have ever had in America. Jefferson was accused of atheism, and the Federalist newspapers said that a vote for him was a vote against God: if the people chose him they could expect "the just vengeance of insulted heaven," and the country would see "dwellings in flames, hoary hairs bathed in blood . . . children writhing on the pike and halberd." The Republicans, in turn, insisted that the Federalists wanted to set up a monarchy and enslave the ordinary people.

In general, the Federalists were favored in New England, where citizens depended upon shipping and trade for their wealth and needed a strong government to negotiate with other nations over trade rights. The Republicans were strongest in the South, where wealth came from farming. Southerners did not want a government which would favor merchants and exporters over farmers.

At bottom, the struggle was seen by a lot of ordinary Americans as one between an elite who would run things as they wished and the more democratic followers of Jefferson. In 1800, Jefferson's Republicans won.

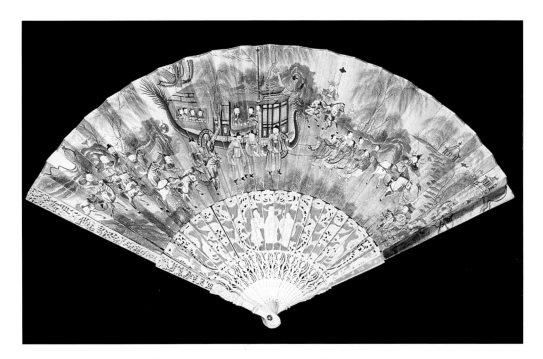

North and South differed in many ways, including their lifestyles and the systems by which they made their livings. Northerners were heavily dependent on commerce, fishing, and shipping for their prosperity. Goods brought in from China and other foreign lands in exchange for American fish, beef, grain, and other products could be sold in the United States for high prices. This delicate Chinese fan was typical of the luxury goods American ships brought back from the Far East.

But there was a joker in the deck. As is the case today, voters from each state chose a number of electors, who in turn selected a president and a vice president. At the time, however, the candidates were not nominated specifically for the offices of president and vice president. The law was that whoever got the most electoral votes would be president; whoever got the second most votes would be vice president. In fact, the Founding Fathers who wrote the Constitution assumed that nobody, aside from Washington, was likely to get a majority of the electoral votes. They pro-

This painting shows a scene of plantation life in the South, possibly in South Carolina. In the background are house, barns, and cabins. In the foreground black slaves are dancing or possibly performing the marriage ceremony of "jumping over the broomstick." The musical instruments are derived from African ones; the stringed instrument is a forerunner of the modern banjo. The South depended on crops like cotton and tobacco for its wealth, with much of the labor provided by slaves.

vided that in such cases that the House of Representatives would decide.

In this election of 1800, Thomas Jefferson and Aaron Burr of New York, who was expected to be vice president, got the same number of votes. Burr—who was on the ticket because he was a clever politician who could draw a lot of northern voters—ought to have stepped aside and let Jefferson be president, as the voters had wished, but he did not. The Federalists still had enough power in Congress to cause a stalemate. They decided to see if somehow they could make hay out of the situation, and refused to elect Jefferson. The one problem was that Burr was an unsavory character, who was nonetheless popular with voters. Later on he would kill Alexander Hamilton in a duel and get involved in a shadowy scheme to set up an empire in the west. Nobody, especially Alexander Hamilton, wanted him for president. Hamilton, in the end, persuaded a few Federalists to come to their senses and vote for Jefferson, as the people wished. Very soon after the election, the Twelfth Amendment was added to the Constitution. The Amendment required electors to vote separately for each, the president and the vice president, and this is the way it is done today.

CHAPTER II

The Louisiana Purchase

Thomas Jefferson, the victor in the fierce contest between the Republicans and the Federalists, was quite a different sort of person from the presidents before him, Washington and Adams. Those two Federalists believed in government by an elite of mostly "well-born" men who had proved themselves by becoming wealthy. They adopted some of the manners of the British aristocracy, dressing in elegant clothes and holding formal parties at which leading figures from law, business, and government mingled.

Thomas Jefferson was a republican who believed that the strength of the country lay in the vast majority of Americans who owned their own farms. Such people had no bosses over them: in those days, before the secret ballot, they could vote as they wished, not how a landlord or employer told them to vote. Jefferson had faith that they would elect the most talented and virtuous men available. To be more like ordinary voters, Jefferson used informal manners. He deliberately dressed in a casual fashion—perhaps too casual a fashion; some emissaries from foreign governments were insulted when they were greeted by a president dressed in a smoking jacket and slippers. He was a rangy man, six feet two in

(above) Thomas Jefferson was a brilliant man with a restless mind: a philosopher, inventor, student of nature, writer, architect. He designed his famous home, Monticello, shown here. It is visited by thousands of people every year.

(right) Jefferson also designed much of the furniture in Monticello. Here is a rotating table Jefferson used to aid him in filing letters and papers.

height, with a freckled face and unruly red hair, and his appearance added to his informal air. When he met with people he sat cocked in his chair on one hip. His informality carried into his presidential duties. Washington and Adams had always given their State of the Nation addresses to Congress in person, but Jefferson thought this practice was too similar to the British king proclaiming his wishes to Parliament. He wrote out his speech and had somebody else read it to Congress.

The capital city, Washington, that Jefferson lived in was even more disheveled than he was. The first homes of the nation's government under the Constitution had been in New York and Philadelphia. But a plan had been worked out for a completely new city to be built in the wilderness, on a piece of land cut out of Maryland, just across the Potomac River from Virginia. A famous architect had been brought in to design the new city, and a capital building for the Congress and a home for the president had been built. But the rest of the city was slow to develop. A few boarding houses had been established for congressmen and other government officials, and government offices were being built. But most of Washington was merely muddy roads through woods and swamps. Strange as it seems, while Jefferson was waiting to be inaugurated president, he lived in a boarding house and did important business in the rough parlor there while other boarders sat around by the fire.

But as yet there was no need for a lot of government buildings, for the government was astonishingly small. The Treasury Department was fairly large because it had to reach out through the country to collect taxes. It had about fifty clerks working in Washington and seven hundred tax collectors and inspectors in the country's seaports. But the entire War Department, which today employs millions of people, consisted of a chief clerk, thirteen ordinary clerks, two messengers, and an army of about four thousand. Partly this was because President Jefferson liked the idea of small government—the people were wise enough to do what needed to be done and government should interfere as little as possible, was his motto. But it is also true that there was simply a lot less for government to do in those days.

It should not be thought, however, that Thomas Jefferson believed that government ought to stay out of things altogether. When you got down to it, Jefferson thought that at least in certain areas the government ought to be strong and active. And it was this part of his philosophy that brought him to one of the most momentous actions of any of the early presidents: the purchase of the Louisiana Territory.

Thomas Jefferson had always been fascinated by the mysterious land that lay west of the Mississippi River. When he was only ten his teacher, James Maury, was involved with plans to explore the land to the west.

In 1833 a Swiss painter named Karl Bodmer traveled through the American west, much of it still unexplored. The paintings he made on his trip are among the finest pictures of the area and are an important source for our knowledge of that time and place. This painting of buffalo and elk on the upper Missouri River shows the country as it must have been at the time of the Louisiana Purchase three decades earlier.

These plans never came to anything, but the young Jefferson's appetite for knowledge of the land out there grew. By the time he became president, explorers and traders had sailed up the Pacific Coast and knew something of the far western lands. For white people, most of the rest of it was a mystery. It was known that there were vast mountains out there, and strange kinds of plants and animals. The best way across it appeared to be via the Missouri River, but nobody knew exactly where the Missouri went or where it began. As Jefferson was growing up, the famous English captain, James Cook, reached what we today call the Pacific Northwest and found the mouth of the Columbia River. Was it possible that the Columbia and Missouri Rivers rose in the mountains near to each other, making a water route across the unknown lands?

Jefferson thus had been possessed by the romance of the vast unknown lands west of the United States. As he rose in power and influence in the country, so too did his vision of a great America grow. He believed that there must be built on the North American continent a nation, or perhaps several nations, sharing one language and driven by the same ideas of freedom and democracy that underlay the United States. Indeed, his thinking went further than that: he believed that in time the Spanish colonies in Central and South America could also be settled by people spreading out from the United States. This vast area, too, would be filled with English-speaking sister republics to the United States. It was to be an Empire of Liberty.

But there were more practical reasons for American interest in the lands across the Mississippi. Over the years since the Revolution, Americans had been crossing the Appalachians to settle the lands there. As we have seen, for these settlers, use of the Mississippi, and the port of New Orleans at its mouth, was absolutely critical. Given the difficulties of carrying freight back across the Appalachians, the only realistic way the westerners had of getting their products to markets on the East Coast, in the Caribbean, and in Europe, was down rivers, like the Ohio, leading to

The Sioux were one of the most powerful tribes in the Great Plains area and were always a threat to explorers and hunters. This Bodmer painting, made during his 1833 trip, shows a Sioux camp very similar to those of 1801, when Jefferson was trying to acquire the land for the United States.

the Mississippi, and then down that great river to New Orleans. Many of these pioneer farmers believed that if the United States could not guarantee their right to use the Mississippi, they would have to break away from the nation, join with some foreign power like Spain, or set up a country of their own which would then take the river and New Orleans by force. Right from the beginning, American governments had been fearful of a breakaway of the west. For Jefferson, the loss of the lands across the Appalachians would end his vision of a vast democratic Republic stretching from the Atlantic to the Pacific.

When Thomas Jefferson became president in 1801, his long-range plan was to get for the United States as much of the lands west of the

Mississippi as he could. There was no rush about that, however. He assumed that Americans would begin drifting across the Mississippi to set up homesteads on the bottomland there, whether they were supposed to or not. Eventually the land would be American, willy nilly.

He was encouraged to believe this by the fact that the land was part of the disintegrating Spanish empire. The Spanish also claimed what is today Florida, along with a slice of land stretching along the Gulf Coast to the west—now coastal Alabama and Mississippi. The British claimed portions of what is now our northwest and were trading for furs with the Indians in the so-called Oregon Territory. Spain, the most powerful nation in Europe during the 1500s, when it was plundering Central and

Another painter traveling through the West at about the same time as Bodmer was Alfred Jacob Miller, who painted a series of pictures of Indians and trappers in 1837. Here a lonely trapper sets out traps for beaver. Beaver skins were one of the great lures of the Northwest.

South America of its wealth in silver and gold, was sliding downward out of power. It was not in a position to challenge the United States directly. Jefferson felt that he could bide his time.

But hardly had Jefferson become president when word drifted into Washington that the Spanish, in a secret pact, were going to turn over New Orleans and the vast Louisiana Territory to France.

This was a different story. Spain was weak. France was now ruled by the Emperor Napoleon Bonaparte. He was a military genius determined to make France a great empire, and he already, through war, had made France the dominant power in Europe. Now he wanted to build a great colonial empire in the Caribbean area. He intended to make New Orleans and Louisiana into a French province.

In order to do so, however, he needed control of the island of Santo Domingo (now Haiti and the Dominican Republic). The island was controlled by rebel blacks, most of them former slaves, led by Toussaint L'Overture. Napoleon began to organize a force to take the island for France.

The situation for Jefferson was growing tense. Still, he did not panic but resisted calls for an invasion of New Orleans. Quietly he began to build up American defenses on the Louisiana borders. More importantly, he ordered Robert Livingston, the American minister in Paris, to see if he could arrange to buy New Orleans and some of the territory around the city from the French.

But the French had still not officially taken over Louisiana. The Spanish were stalling. Furthermore, the French were having trouble conquering Santo Domingo. The problem was not so much Toussaint L'Overture; it was instead the deadly yellow fever, which was killing French soldiers by the thousands.

Then, suddenly, the Spanish commander in New Orleans revoked the Americans' "right of deposit" in that city. The right of deposit meant essentially that Americans could use New Orleans as a place to transfer

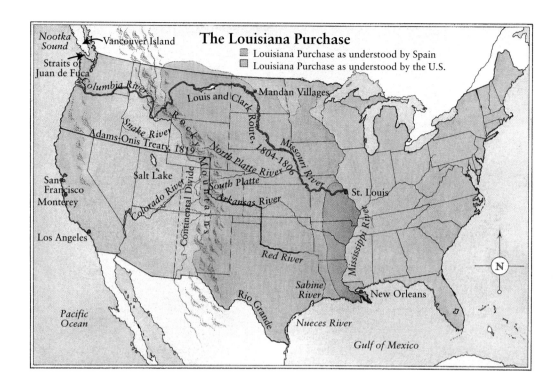

The Louisiana Purchase

■ Louisiana Purchase as understood by Spain
■ Louisiana Purchase as understood by the U.S.

goods from Mississippi riverboats to ocean-going ships. Now many Americans, especially western farmers and merchants who needed to ship goods through New Orleans, were up in arms and ready to take the city by force. Jefferson knew that was not wise, for it would push America into a war with France, at the moment the most powerful nation in Europe. He calmed people's fears and once more settled in to wait things out.

Meanwhile, things were worse than ever for the French on Santo Domingo. Yellow fever continued to sweep like a deadly scythe through Napoleon's troops there. By October 1802, over twenty-four thousand French soldiers had died, mostly from yellow fever but many in battle with the black troops. Then the French commander died of disease. Back in Paris, Napoleon was beginning to lose faith in his idea of a great colonial empire in the Caribbean.

Jefferson did not yet know this. But he was confident that before long, war between the British and the French would once more break out. The French would then be too busy at home to worry about Louisiana. Jefferson hoped to take advantage of that. He now sent a second emissary, James Monroe, to Paris, to speed up negotiations to buy New Orleans. He also wanted to include in the purchase Florida and the stretches along the Gulf Coast east of New Orleans held by Spain. He assumed that Spain had turned this territory over to France, along with New Orleans, as part of the secret treaty. (In fact, that had not happened.)

When Monroe arrived, he discovered that on that very day, the French foreign minister, Talleyrand, anticipating the transfer from Spain to France, had offered to sell the *entire* Louisiana Territory to the United States. Napoleon had given up on Santo Domingo and was preparing once more to fight the English. He could not very well defend New Orleans while he was fighting elsewhere; furthermore, he would need money for his war. Without New Orleans, the rest of the Louisiana Territory was useless to Napoleon. Why not sell the whole thing for more money than he would get for New Orleans alone and rid himself of an indefensible colony at the same time?

The American emissaries, Monroe and Livingston, were stunned and for a moment hesitated. But quickly they came to their senses: the opportunity was too great to be missed. Unfortunately, they had authority from the government back in Washington only to buy New Orleans and the Spanish Florida colonies for not more than $10 million. Napoleon wanted $15 million for the whole Louisiana Purchase. Monroe and Livingston had only a hazy idea of what they were negotiating for. Some people believed that there was a vast inland sea in the middle of the territory. Others believed that it was filled with strange sorts of animals. Nearly everybody hoped that there was some kind of a water passage through it, probably via the Missouri River, to the Pacific Ocean. But whatever was

Napoleon Bonaparte, one of the great conquerors of modern times. Needing money for his war with England, Bonaparte sold Louisiana to the United States. It was a great bargain for America.

out there, Monroe and Livingston knew they had to buy the land, and they agreed to the price of $15 million—less than three cents an acre for what would prove to be hugely valuable land, today worth billions of dollars.

News of the Louisiana Purchase reached the United States on July 4, 1803. Most Americans were overjoyed—the nation had suddenly become one of the largest in the world—and Jefferson was ecstatic. But not everybody was so enthusiastic. The Federalists, in particular, grumbled. One of them said, "I believe it will be the greatest curse that could ever befall us. Citizens will be removed to the immense distance of two or three thousand miles from the Capitol, where they will scarcely ever feel the rays of the Central government. Their affections will become alienated; they will gradually begin to view us as strangers." Among other things, the Federalists were concerned that the new western lands would quickly fill up with settlers; new states would be created, and in time they would overbalance the older states along the eastern seaboard. (In fact, this did not happen: most of the states carved out of the Louisiana Purchase remain thinly settled by modern standards.)

Even Jefferson had some doubts about whether the Constitution permitted him to make this grand deal. The Constitution said nothing about buying huge tracts of land; it did not forbid it, either. In any case, the Senate ratified the treaty, and later scholars have agreed that the Louisiana Purchase was legal under the Constitution.

It is ironic that a man who became president determined to make the U.S. government smaller and less powerful ended up doing something that had the opposite effect. The Louisiana Purchase forced the government to take on new jobs in order to deal with the newly acquired land. The Indians, of course, owned the land, and it was necessary for the U.S. Government to expand its techniques for providing legal cover for dispossessing the Indians. That is, new treaties had to be negotiated—and when negotiations failed, imposed—with the tribes so that Americans who wished to be law-abiding could feel that they were so. Additionally, much of the area that the U.S. Government believed to be included in the purchase was not thought so by the Spanish government. Northwest of the purchase, England and Russia had territorial claims as well. Thus the acquisition of Louisiana required a large expansion of the work of Jefferson's administration—just the opposite of his "small government" vision.

Moreover, the Louisiana Purchase forced Americans to think more nationally. The land out there did not belong to individual states, but to the government as a whole: The pioneers who wanted to settle it, the trappers who wanted to hunt beaver there, the traders who wanted to deal with the Indians found themselves under no state government, just the national one.

CHAPTER III

The Lewis and Clark Expedition

The Louisiana Purchase was a great thing, most Americans agreed. Now they had to find out exactly what it was that the nation had bought. Nobody even knew, except vaguely, what the boundaries of the area were. The claim ran north to the headwaters of the Missouri River, that is to say, the point where a tiny stream which would become the wide Missouri rose from the ground. But nobody knew where that was. The western boundary was the Rockies, or the Shining Mountains, as they were often called, but nobody knew exactly where the Rockies were, either. Americans were intensely curious about this vast area, and inevitably, their imaginations filled in a lot of blank spaces on the map. Unfortunately, a lot of their planning was based on an imaginative geography of their new acquisition.

One error people made was to assume that the unknown lands to the west were all like the country just across the Mississippi, which they knew about. The area had rich soil and was cut by broad rivers, like the Arkansas and the Missouri, which a few explorers had traveled along. However, much of the new territory was desertlike, without significant rivers.

Another error was that although very few whites had even seen the Rockies, much less set foot in them, there was a widespread belief that they consisted of a long, relatively low ridge running north and south which, Americans wishfully hoped, was broken in spots, where pioneers could slip through easily to the Pacific Ocean. In fact, the Rockies were at points over twelve thousand feet above sea level, two hundred miles wide, and consisted of a writhing mass of ridges, peaks, and valleys which even today are a challenge to climbers. Furthermore, they were unbroken from Alaska to Mexico and were in places flanked by yet other mountains, like the Sierra Nevada range, which runs like a spine down much of California. If Americans had had any idea of how formidable the Rocky Mountains were, they might have lost heart at the outset.

But the mountains and the deserts were not the only obstacles standing in the way of American hopes of pushing into the new land. As it happened, the territory was already occupied by tens of thousands of warlike Indians, who had no intention of letting whites simply take over their land. The cultures of these western Indians varied a great deal. In the South there were the Pueblo dwellers of what is now New Mexico, who lived in adobe apartment buildings and grew corn for their main food. In the Northwest were rich and powerful tribes who carved the famous totem poles and built great canoes for war or to hunt sea creatures, like walruses.

The main group of Indians occupying the Louisiana Territory were the Indians of the Great Plains. Today when we think of Indians, we often think of these plains Indians, for they are the ones shown most often in movie and television dramas of the Old West. These were fierce, hard-riding Indians equipped with rifles, who lived in tepee villages. In fact, these plains Indians were unusual. Most American Indians had no horses and few guns, and lived in semipermanent villages—along the seashore in the summer, perhaps, and in wooded hunting regions in the winter—in dwellings made of skins, mats, or sheets of bark stretched over pole frames. The Indians on the east side of the Mississippi, still very numerous when Jefferson became president in 1801, grew much of their own food, like corn, beans, and squash, although they hunted and fished as well.

The Indians of the Louisiana Territory had once lived this way, too. But in the 1500s they had come into contact with the Spanish explorers and settlers pushing north from Mexico. (For the story of Spanish Colonialism in America see the volume *Hispanic America, Texas, and the Mexican War* in this series.) The Spanish brought with them two things that would transform Indian life on the plains: horses and European diseases. We often believe that the Indians were defeated by European guns, but in fact it was diseases—brought by the French, Dutch, English, and other Europeans as well as the Spanish—that were the Indians' worst enemy. These diseases, like smallpox, measles, even mumps, were dangerous to Europeans and killed millions of them; but over the centuries Europeans had acquired a certain amount of immunity to such diseases, and most of them survived epidemics. The Indians had no such immunity. When a disease like smallpox struck an Indian village it was likely to kill 90 percent of the people—or even all of them—and then sweep on to the next village, where it would do the same. We are not sure how many Indians lived on the Great Plains before the whites came with their diseases, but the population ran to hundreds of thousands. By the time of the Louisiana Purchase they numbered in the tens of thousands. The Mandans, for example, probably numbered between six thousand and ten thousand in the early 1700s; a hundred years later they were down to 1500, and by the mid-nineteenth century only a couple of hundred remained.

But if disease was ruinous to the plains Indians, the horse gave them a brief golden age. Horses like to roam, and Indians easily managed to steal or capture some. In 1680, during a revolt of the Pueblo Indians of the Southwest against the Spanish conquerors, the Indians took a large number of horses. Both through trade and capture, horses quickly spread north up the plains into Canada, until almost every tribe had them.

Horses made it possible for the Indians to run down and kill the buffalo (properly called bison) that swarmed by the millions in huge herds over the plains. Horses also made it possible for the Indians to carry big loads of food and supplies as they traveled across the plains. Many tribes gave up their agricultural way of life, with their semipermanent villages

Americans did not realize how rough the newly acquired Louisiana Territory was. The Great Plains, which took up much of the northern half, was occupied by Indians who had become great horsemen. These Indians followed the buffalo, which gave them much of what they needed to exist. This picture of a buffalo hunt was painted by yet another famous artist of the West, George Catlin. It was painted some years after the Lewis and Clark Expedition, but Indian hunting technique had not changed much.

and agricultural economy, for a life regulated by the migration of the plains buffalo. Buffalo richly supplied them with almost everything they needed: food, robes, skins, even fuel, for they could burn buffalo dung for fires.

By the time of the Louisiana Purchase, the Great Plains of the west was filled with migrating Indian tribes, who frequently raided each other's camps for horses and fought over rights to land. The Indians in the northern area of the plains, up toward Canada, tended to follow their traditional settled agricultural cultures, but they frequently traded for guns with the British, who had claimed Canada. As guns spread throughout the plains tribes, their warfare grew more deadly. Tribes that did not have guns were desperate for them and would do almost anything to get them.

The Indians of the Great Plains were warlike and were eager to get guns from whites. Here is a Bodmer painting of an Assiniboine-Cree attack on a Piegan camp, outside the walls of Fort McKenzie. Artists often imagine such scenes of battle, but Bodmer actually witnessed this fight.

The Indians moving about the Great Plains would prove to Americans as great a barrier to the settlement of the Louisiana Purchase lands as the mountains and the deserts. Long after the railroad had made travel across the Great Plains relatively comfortable and easy, the Indians continued to assert their claims to the land—often violently.

Jefferson, as we have seen, had always been intensely curious about this great unexplored American interior, and he had developed his romantic vision of making it part of a vast democratic empire. But he also had more practical purposes in mind.

For one, given his faith in independent farm families as the heart of American democracy, he naturally wanted to make sure there was plenty of good farmland for them to spread into. It was crucial to know what the land in the Louisiana Territory was like and where the best farmland lay.

For another, beaver fur was still much in demand, not only in America, but even more in Europe, as the raw material for felt for making hats, a fashion that had persisted for two hundred years. The British had already crossed Canada to the Pacific and were trading millions of dollars worth of beaver fur and other skins. British fur traders and trappers were sliding down from Canada to make claims in what are now Washington and Oregon. Jefferson wanted not only to take over this fur trade for Americans, but also to stop the British from making good on their claims to the lands of the northwest. Indeed, Jefferson even hoped that the purchase would give Americans a toehold on the Pacific Ocean and the rich China trade.

Finally, the few sketchy reports Americans had had about these vast western lands suggested that the Missouri River began not far from the headwaters of the Columbia River, which drained into the Pacific Ocean at what is now the border of Washington and Oregon. If this was the case—and everybody believed it must be so—it would be possible to travel to the Pacific by boat from where the Missouri joined the Mississippi at St. Louis, then a rough frontier town. There would have to be a portage across land between the two rivers, but that was probably, people thought, short. In fact, the two river systems were divided by an almost impassable chunk of the towering Rockies, requiring a portage of 340 miles. Only the Indians knew that, however, and Jefferson remained optimistic that a route to the Pacific could be found. Attempts had been made to explore the area, but they had failed.

Inevitably, not long after he had become president, Jefferson began to think about a new expedition to explore the Louisiana Territory. As it happened, he had living with him as his personal secretary, a young man named Meriwether Lewis. Lewis came from a well-to-do Virginia family and had had some schooling. He had also served as a captain in the army on the frontier, where he had had to deal with Indians. He was a restless man who was not always bound by routine army discipline. He was ideal for Jefferson's plans.

Even before Jefferson knew that he would be able to buy the whole Louisiana Territory, he had started grooming Lewis for the task of exploring it. He had Lewis tutored in zoology and botany so he would be able to recognize new species of plants and animals when he came across them. Lewis also learned how to fix his position by the stars, in order to accurately

Meriwether Lewis, who, with his friend William Clark, led the famous expedition through the Louisiana Territory to the Pacific.

locate the unknown rivers and mountains he would discover. Lewis was very excited by the opportunity, and he persuaded a friend and fellow officer, William Clark, to go with him. Clark was officially termed second in command of the expedition, but Lewis treated him as an equal. While preparations were going on, word came of the Louisiana Purchase.

Jefferson laid out several missions for Meriwether Lewis. The most important was to find a water passage through the continent to the Pacific Ocean. It was assumed that he would travel up the Missouri River until it gave out, they hoped, somewhere in the Rocky Mountains. From here, they also hoped, Lewis would find a short overland portage to the headwaters of the Columbia River. No white man had ever been all the way up the Missouri, nor all the way up the Columbia from the Pacific Ocean; nobody knew for sure what they would be like.

In addition, Lewis was supposed to describe and, if possible, collect samples of the strange plants and animals he was bound to come across and bring back as many as he could. Jefferson was much interested in science, and he wanted to know, as much as a matter of curiosity as for practical use, what sort of life the vast unexplored land contained. The explorers would also map the countryside they passed through.

Finally, Lewis and Clark were expected to establish some sort of diplomatic relations with the Indians. Many Americans had little interest in the Indians and merely wanted to shove them out of the way in order to take over the land. Not all Americans felt that way, however. President Jefferson was of two minds about the Indians. On one hand, he sympathized with them and wished he could treat them fairly. But he believed that the only way the Indians could survive the expansion of American culture was to become part of it.

The best thing for everybody, Jefferson decided, was to integrate the Indians into American society. They would be turned into farmers, their children would go to school to learn American ways, and eventually they would intermarry with the whites and be entirely absorbed. To get this program started, Lewis and Clark were supposed to impress the Indians with the irresistible might of the United States—indeed, it was hoped that some important chiefs could be persuaded to come to Washington to see for themselves how mighty the chief there was.

On top of these goals, there began to arise in Lewis's mind a grand scheme from which Americans, including himself, would benefit. He wanted to redirect the Indians' trade away from the English and Russians to the north and instead bring these furs and skins over the Rockies to the Pacific Ocean; from there they would be shipped to China where they could be traded for valuable goods like silk and tea.

Lewis and Clark planned to take a small group, large enough for protection but not so large as to make the Indians feel threatened. In May 1804, forty-five men—most of them soldiers—started up the Missouri River from St. Louis in a large keelboat, which could be rowed or sailed if the wind were good, and some smaller boats. Thus began one of the most remarkable adventures ever undertaken by Americans, or indeed by anyone anywhere. This small party was to travel nearly three thousand miles through vast prairies, across one of the world's greatest mountain ranges, all the while at risk from Indians, who vastly outnumbered them and many of whom had never seen whites before. They were to live off the land and build their own shelter against the vicious winters of the northern plains. And they did it all. Again and again they boldly walked into Indian villages where they could have been easy prey, to trade with the Indians for food and horses and to present them with gifts meant to make it clear to the Indians that they would do well to establish trading relations with the Americans.

For weeks the little party struggled up the Missouri, hunting in the prairie along the river for deer and buffalo. They spent the first winter in cabins they built next to a village of friendly Mandan Indians, in the middle of what is now North Dakota. Slowly they came to understand the Indians better.

(above) The Lewis and Clark Expedition spent a winter in huts near a Mandan Indian Village. They became friendly with the Mandans and learned much about them. This is the interior of a Mandan earth lodge painted some years later by Karl Bodmer.

(left) Another painting by Karl Bodmer, showing a Mandan Indian girl dressed in deerskins and wearing ear pendants and a necklace of beads.

Contrary to what Jefferson had hoped, the Indians had no interest in giving up their cultures to become farmers and be absorbed into the white population. There were in the northern plains alone some twenty Indian groups, which in turn were divided into many subgroups. These groups had their own rituals for marriage and death, spoke a number of different languages and dialects, and were entangled with each other in complex shifting alliances broken by raids and open warfare.

Lewis and Clark came to understand much about the ways of the plains Indians, but they never really grasped the idea that, although the Indians were interested in trading with the whites for guns and other items, they wanted nothing more than to be left in peace to go about their business as they always had.

This Bodmer painting shows Mandans using dog sleds to haul things from place to place.

Yet another Bodmer painting shows the Mandan dance of the Buffalo, meant to ensure a good hunt.

Nonetheless, Lewis, in particular, proved to be a very skilled diplomat in very trying circumstances. In some cases he found people who could interpret for him, but often he had to use the sign language that the plains Indians all knew to do his trading and persuade chiefs to make the long trip to Washington. Some of the Indians, especially the Sioux, were hostile to whites, but so well did Lewis manage that the party was never seriously attacked. For the most part, he was able to trade with the Indians for the food, horses, and other things the expedition needed.

When the spring of 1805 finally arrived, the party set off once again, traveling at various times by boat, on horseback, and on foot. With the help of some Shoshone Indians, they struggled up over the Rockies and

The Lewis and Clark expedition excited the interest of Americans. Various reports and descriptions of the trip were issued by members of the expedition and by others. This drawing from such a report shows Lewis and Clark meeting with a group of Indians.

then made the long, rugged portage to the headwaters of the Columbia. They were still not safe, for the Columbia dropped rapidly out of the mountains and was filled with tumultuous rapids which constantly threatened to dash the boats into the rocks. But they survived, and on November 7, 1805, they reached the mouth of the Columbia River where it emptied into the Pacific.

They could not cross back over the Rockies in the dead of winter, so they built a rough fort and stayed at the mouth of the Columbia until spring. Then they began the arduous trip back over the mountains. The trip home was at times even worse than the trip going west had been, but once they reached the Missouri and could travel downstream, things went more easily. In September 1806, they swept into St. Louis. They had

Another drawing illustrating a report on the Lewis and Clark expedition, this one showing the men building huts for one of their encampments. The expedition spent one winter in huts near the Mandans, and another winter along the Columbia River, waiting for warm weather before starting home.

been gone for two-and-a-half years and had traveled three thousand miles through some of the roughest country in the world. Incredibly, they had lost only one man, Sergeant Charles Floyd, who died of illness early in the trip.

The great adventure was finally over. Paradoxically, it had been, in some ways, a failure. On his return, Lewis was forced to report to President Jefferson that there was no easy water route across the continent; to the contrary, the way was virtually impassable. Nor had Lewis and Clark been able to convince the Indians to bring themselves under the rule of the Great White Father in Washington. As more and more whites pressed into the plains, first to trap and trade, and then to farm, relations with the Indians went from bad to worse. There would be no great trading scheme to ship beaver pelts out to China, and the prospects for peaceful relations had scarcely been improved.

But the effect of the Lewis and Clark expedition on Americans was electric. The great adventure had captured the imagination of the people. The expedition had hardly got back to St. Louis when small parties of trappers and traders began to set out into Indian territory after the beaver that Lewis had seen in such abundance.

Furthermore, the sampling of animals and plants that Lewis sent back, and especially his descriptions of novel species unknown in the east, like grizzly bears, proved to be of great value to scientists. There was now no doubt that the United States would expand into the west.

Like the Louisiana Purchase itself, the Lewis and Clark Expedition had a strongly nationalizing effect on Americans. It had been an American adventure, through fabulous territory that was now theirs. Accounts of the trip written by members of the expedition were widely read. Americans were proud of the spirit Lewis and Clark's band of courageous explorers had shown.

CHAPTER IV

The States versus the Federal Government: The Supreme Court Steps In

When the Founding Fathers were debating the Constitution in 1787, one of the biggest issues was how much power ought to be given to the Federal government and how much ought to be left to the states. At that time, most Americans thought of themselves as citizens of their home states, rather than as Americans. It is somewhat similar to the situation today, where we recognize that we are members of the United Nations, but certainly think of ourselves first and foremost as Americans rather than as citizens of the world. So did people in those days think of themselves first and foremost as Virginians, Georgians, Rhode Islanders, New Yorkers. True, by the time Thomas Jefferson became president, the idea of putting the nation first was growing; but it was a long way from being wholly accepted.

Thus, even though the Constitution seemed to have set the Federal government over the states in many matters, a lot of Americans still felt that in most cases the national government ought not to be able to override the states. Indeed, many believed that the states ought to have the final word. In truth, although the Constitution was a work of genius, the Founding Fathers had not been able to spell out in detail answers to every question that might come up, and inevitably there were areas that the Constitution was not clear about.

The problem was, who would have the final say when questions came up about who had power over a certain matter? Who had the power to declare laws passed by Congress unconstitutional? Somebody had to, for if nobody could declare acts of Congress unconstitutional, then the Congress could do whatever it liked, regardless of the Constitution and its important Bill of Rights. This was the central issue in the famous case of *Marbury v. Madison,* which the Supreme Court heard in 1803. In deciding this case, John Marshall, the most influential Supreme Court justice of all time, said that the Supreme Court had this power, because it had to have it to settle cases like Marbury. (Readers interested in more details on this important case can consult *Creating the Constitution* in this series.)

Chief Justice John Marshall, a formidable figure who did much, through his rulings, to establish the Supreme Court as a power in American government, well beyond anything that the Founding Fathers had expected.

Marbury v. Madison seemed to make the point that the Supreme Court needed to have the power to invalidate congressional laws that seemed contrary to the Constitution. But what about cases in which Congress passed laws that were contrary to the laws of a *state?* Should not the states have the final say in those areas?

During the first decades of the 1800s, the Supreme Court ruled on a number of cases concerning state versus federal power. Once again, John Marshall played a major role in these decisions. We will look at four of these critically important cases.

One of these was the Yazoo land case, officially known as *Fletcher v. Peck.* It involved an extraordinary public swindle that one historian has called "the greatest corrupt real estate deal in American history." In 1795 Georgia still included the territory all the way to the Mississippi River. Some land speculators bribed almost everybody in the Georgia legislature to permit the state to sell the speculators 35 million acres of Yazoo

Americans were land hungry, always pressing into new areas. This cabin was typical of the rough homes that settlers created for themselves during the frontier period. Everybody assumed you could always make money dealing in land. The Yazoo case was a prime example of the frantic land speculation of the early national era.

Territory, in what is today Alabama and Mississippi, for a very low price, about seventy acres for a dollar. Naturally, when the people of Georgia found out about the Yazoo deal they were outraged, and in 1796 they elected a new legislature. This legislature canceled the deal. However, in the meantime, the speculators had been selling their land to others for big profit, and these people were selling it to yet other people at more profit. After the Yazoo deal was overturned by the Georgia legislature, everyone's title to their plots fell into question, and a great many people faced the loss of their farms and all the money they had invested.

Inevitably, somebody sued. The argument was this: the Constitution said that no state government could pass any "Law impairing the Obligation of Contracts"; that is, they could not interfere with contracts. According to this argument, the legislature of Georgia, in selling the Yazoo land in the first place, had entered into a contract with the buyers and therefore could not go back on the deal. One big question in the case was whether a public law like the land sale one was truly a contract. John Marshall and his Supreme Court ruled that it was and that the reversal of that law by a later legislature had impaired the original contract, so the Yazoo land deal had to be allowed.

The net result of this ruling was to make it very difficult for state legislatures to change their minds on certain matters, especially when people's property was involved—even when the public welfare could be helped by a change of law, as in the Yazoo case. It was a questionable call by the Supreme Court because usually when fraud can be proven, contracts can be canceled. But Marshall was determined to clip the wings of state legislatures which he, like many Federalists, thought were unruly, inconsistent, often irrational, and in need of some discipline from the central government. And he wanted to be sure that the U.S. Constitution protected private property rights.

A second case also touching on the law of contracts came up in 1819, *Dartmouth College v. Woodward*. It involved the idea of the "corporation." Corporations had existed for centuries. Many had been formed by investors in England to build up settlements in the new lands of America in the 1600s. These colonial corporations were usually authorized by the British government. They granted the investors a large piece of land in America on which to build their settlement and established rules about how the settlement was to be run. Kings, queens, and Parliament reserved the right to change these rules, and often did.

By the early 1800s a new type of corporation was coming into existence. This was the business corporation so familiar to us today. These corporations were established by private individuals who got charters from state governments. These charters permitted investors to do certain things—for example, build a toll bridge over a river, operate a steamboat, start a factory for the purpose of making textiles. These business operations were seen as "private" corporations, rather than public ones as the earlier ones had been.

The Dartmouth College case began when the New Hampshire legislature decided it wanted to turn Dartmouth into a state college. The trustees of Dartmouth fought back, and eventually the suit landed in the Supreme Court. The question was whether a legislature could change the terms of the original corporate grant, in this case one given by the king way back in 1769. Some said yes: Dartmouth College was not a private corporation but a public one. It was not there to make a profit for private investors, but was a charitable institution with a public function— that is, educating the young citizens of New Hampshire.

John Marshall disagreed. He said that a corporate charter was obviously a contract. Dartmouth College, he announced, was a private institution. Therefore, the legislature of New Hampshire could not change the "contract" under which the college had been established. The effect of the Dartmouth case was to restrict the state governments' ability to control and regulate private corporations. Though states found ways of getting around the extreme "laissez-faire" (hands off) position of

Dartmouth College in the early days. John Marshall's opinion in the case involving Dartmouth was important in establishing the rights of private corporations.

Dartmouth College v. Woodward, and of course Congress can regulate business under the interstate commerce clause of the Constitution, the effect of Marshall's decision was to make the U.S. government the prime protector of private property rights. The decision enshrined those rights, making them as important as, for instance, freedom of religion and press. Once again Marshall and his fellow justices had enhanced the power of the U.S. government by restricting the powers of the states.

A third case decided by the Marshall Court was *M'Culloch v. Maryland.* It is considered by many historians to be the most important case ever decided by the U.S. Supreme Court. We need to look at the background to see what makes it so crucial to us.

Back in 1789, George Washington's Secretary of the Treasury, Alexander Hamilton, had decided that the government ought to set up a national bank to solve a number of very real problems the brand-new nation was facing. At the time, opponents of Hamilton's idea for a national bank argued that the Constitution did not give the government the power to create any such thing. The Constitution, said Hamilton's opponents like Thomas Jefferson, set out the specific powers that the national government was to have. These were the "enumerated powers" such as: to declare war, raise taxes, borrow money, and so forth. Nothing was said about the power to establish a bank.

President George Washington was very concerned about this constitutional issue. He asked his aids their opinions on it, including Hamilton himself. Hamilton pointed out that while it was true that the Constitution did not explicitly give the federal government the right to start a bank, it did say that the Congress could do things that were *necessary and proper* to carry out the duties that the Constitution did explicitly authorize. For example, the Constitution did not specifically say that Congress could design and purchase military uniforms. However, the Constitution did say that Congress could establish an army and navy; uniforms surely would be a necessary and proper part of establishing a military force. These powers growing out of the enumerated powers we call "implied powers."

Hamilton insisted that a national bank was necessary and proper to fulfill various duties the Constitution had enumerated as belonging to Congress, like collecting taxes and paying the debts of the nation. Hamilton's opponents said that, to the contrary, a national bank was not necessary—these things could be done in other ways. It all came down to how you defined the word *necessary*. Did it mean something essential, something you couldn't do without? Or did it mean merely that it would be helpful to getting something done? So far as Hamilton and his supporters were concerned, a thing could be considered necessary if it were

Alexander Hamilton, George Washington's Secretary of the Treasury, had pressed Congress to establish a national bank in order to encourage commerce. There had always been considerable opposition to the bank, which many people said was unconstitutional, as the Constitution said nothing about establishing a national bank. In settling the M'Culloch v. Maryland case involving the bank, Marshall interpreted the "necessary and proper" clause broadly, setting a precedent still followed today.

merely helpful. Washington agreed with Hamilton, so did Congress, and a national bank was established.

But there was still a great deal of opposition to the bank, and in 1816 several states, including Maryland, decided to put a tax on the paper notes issued by the branches of the national bank in their states. The tax would have to be paid by the federal government. The whole thing boiled up into the famous lawsuit of *M'Culloch v. Maryland,* which landed in the Supreme Court. The lawyers for Maryland put up the old argument that the Constitution had not authorized Congress to establish a bank in the first place. The Constitution, they said, had been set up by the states, and thus the states must have the final power.

In his decision John Marshall said, first of all, that, in fact, the Constitution had not been set up by the states. It had instead been set up by the American people as a whole, when they had voted to ratify it. "The government," Marshall wrote in his decision, "proceeds directly from the people; is 'ordained and established' in the name of the people. . . ."

He then got around to that tiny but immensely powerful phrase "necessary and proper." What, exactly, did it mean? John Marshall said that, as commonly used, the word *necessary* means "that one thing is convenient, or useful, or essential to another." Of course, there is a great difference between convenient and essential, but Marshall chose to lump them together. In this, he was agreeing with what Hamilton had said back in 1789. Marshall summed up his opinion in one of the most famous statements in American law, this way:

> Let the end be legitimate, let it be within the scope of the constitution, and all means which are appropriate, which are plainly adapted to that end, which are not prohibited, but consist with the letter and spirit of the constitution, are constitutional . . . .

This was an extremely broad statement, for it did seem to allow the national government to do almost anything it wanted. It was not infinitely broad, however: the Congress could not pass laws under the "necessary and proper" clause that were "prohibited" by or contrary to the "spirit of the constitution."

For example, the "necessary and proper" clause in the Constitution could not be used to require states to set up school systems. Nor could it be used to forbid the states to build highways and bridges within their own borders.

Chief Justice John Marshall and other members of the Supreme Court were what are known as "loose constructionists." This means that they "constructed," or interpreted, the Constitution broadly. To put it another way, loose constructionists said that the Constitution *implied* a lot of things that were not actually *enumerated* in it. They believed that the Founding Fathers, in writing the Constitution, knew that they could not plan for everything that might come up: the Constitution, so these loose constructionists claimed, had to be interpreted broadly to allow the government to deal with novel questions.

One such innovation, which would lead to another important case, was the steamboat. We remember that in a time before railroads, when roads were mostly muddy, rocky trails through the woods, transportation of bulky goods over any distance had to be by water. Particularly important to Americans was the network of rivers running through the land: the Hudson-Mohawk chain that reached from New York City almost to the Great Lakes; the Delaware, which connected Trenton and Philadelphia to the sea; and most especially the Ohio, Mississippi, and their tributaries, which carried people and freight out of the vast lands across the Appalachians to New Orleans and from there to the rest of the world. The problem with rivers was that it was easy enough to go downstream; but going back upstream against the current by means of oars, poles, or sails, was arduous and time-consuming. It might take months to get a keelboat from New Orleans back up the Mississippi and the Ohio to Pittsburgh. (The development of our early transportation system is discussed in *Andrew Jackson's America* in this series.)

The idea of the steamboat had interested inventors for a long time, and by the late 1780s John Fitch had managed to develop a workable steamboat, which briefly provided a rather unreliable service on the Delaware River. In 1807 Robert Fulton, with an improved version of the steamboat, began regular service on the Hudson River from New York to Albany. Suddenly steamboats were everywhere; soon the trip from New Orleans to Pittsburgh was being made in a week. The coming of the

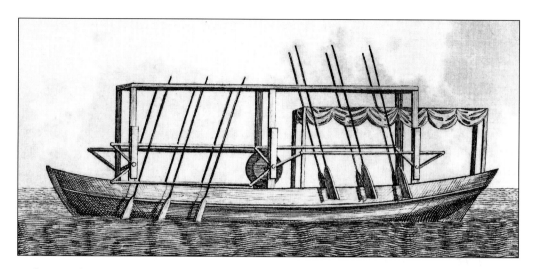

John Fitch's original idea for the steamboat was to power oars by a steam engine. It worked and, for a while, provided service on the Delaware river

Fitch's steamboat was soon superseded by a better system, which used a steam-driven paddle wheel. These paddle wheelers proved to be a great success, and soon they were everywhere. This is the Wm. Cutting, *one of Robert Fulton's boats that operated on the Hudson River.*

steamboat was immensely important to the development of the United States, especially the lands to the west.

Of course, there was a great deal of money to be made in running steamboats. Fulton, his partners, and later on their heirs managed to wangle from the New York State legislature the *sole* right to run steamboats up and down the Hudson River—a monopoly, as it is called. Needless to say, there were a lot of complaints about this. People said that there ought to be competing steamboat lines on the Hudson to drive prices down. Inevitably, other promoters set up steamboat lines in defiance of the monopoly New York State had granted to the first group. These competitors claimed that the power to "regulate Commerce . . . among the several states" was given by the Constitution to the national government, not to the states. Naturally, the men holding the monopoly granted by the state sued the "illegal" competitors, and there eventually landed before the Supreme Court yet another now-famous case, called *Gibbons v. Ogden.*

The case was quite complicated, and we do not have to get into all the ins and outs of it here. The main point is that Chief Justice Marshall took a broad view of the Constitution and construed the commerce clause in the Constitution loosely. He said that the word *commerce* did not just apply to "business," but to other related matters as well, like transportation. While the states could regulate commerce that was wholly within a state and concerned that state alone, anything that involved other states, or the interests of the nation generally, could be regulated only by the national government.

In these two cases, *M'Culloch v. Maryland* and *Gibbons v. Ogden,* Marshall and his supporters on the Supreme Court were well aware that they were setting up important rules for the nation. Of course, later Supreme Courts could reverse these rules and the people could amend the Constitution, but Marshall knew that it was hard to change precedents once they were established. Marshall had a clear idea of how he thought the nation should go, and he deliberately put that idea into his court decisions. He said that "strict constructionists" who would abide by the exact wording of the Constitution would "explain away the constitution of our country, and leave it a magnificent structure, indeed, to look at, but totally unfit for use."

This, then, was Marshall's idea: that the Constitution had to be loosely interpreted, so it could allow the government to deal with new situations. The net effect of Marshall's decisions was to permit Congress to do a great many things that the Constitution never mentioned. Did he go beyond the intentions of the Founding Fathers when they wrote the Constitution? Some, like James Madison and Thomas Jefferson, said he did and Madison, after all, had played a major role in its writing. But most historians today agree with John Marshall and regard him as one of the great figures in American history, as important in his way as Washington and Lincoln in theirs.

Summing up, we can see that in the early years the Supreme Court, along with the Congress and the president, were laying out a lot of the ground rules for the new American government. It is unlikely that many of the Founding Fathers had intended that the Court play such a large role in this. Nonetheless, most historians believe that in the very early years of the nation's founding, the Supreme Court made the right decisions. These cases came to them and they had to decide the Constitutional issues that were raised. Of course, if different men had sat on the Supreme Court at the time, they might well have decided differently; indeed, a minority of historians believe that the cases we have been looking at were not properly decided. John Marshall and his five associate justices firmly believed in strong national government. In all four of the cases we have looked at, the Court showed its belief that the Constitution required the Court to clip the wings of the state governments and expand the powers of Congress. At the same time, Marshall's decisions protected private property rights at the expense of what state governments thought were the public needs of their citizens. That Marshall's decisions have remained the law of the land ever since his day shows that he picked his cases wisely and argued them convincingly. Most historians today believe that Marshall was most wise because his interpretation of the Constitution helped to give the national government the strength it would need for the difficult times ahead.

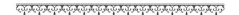

CHAPTER V

The War of 1812

Historians have long argued over the causes of the War of 1812 and whether it ought to have been fought at all. The causes of this rather formless war were partly psychological and its results were partly psychological, too. But they were nonetheless important, for the United States came out of the War of 1812 with a much more solid sense of itself as one nation than it had when it went into it.

The war was, essentially, a by-product of a long and bitter struggle between Great Britain and France. Under Napoleon Bonaparte, France had become possibly the mightiest nation on earth, the master of much of Europe. Napoleon's ambitions were boundless: he intended to make himself emperor of as much of the western world as he could.

The one nation able to stand up to France was England. It had the finest navy ever built in its day and its armies were also strong and superbly trained. From the mid-1790s on, these two nations were almost constantly at war, with short intervals of peace.

The United States had complex and conflicting relationships with both these nations. England, of course, was the "mother country" to the United States. Most Americans spoke English, used a system of law derived from England, worshipped in churches with English roots, and perhaps just as important, for two centuries had counted on trade with Great Britain for much of their prosperity.

Yet America had recently fought a long and bloody revolution to rid itself of English rule; England, to many Americans, was not just the mother country and an important trading partner, it was also the enemy.

American attitudes toward the French were equally contradictory. The French had given America critically important help during the Revolution—the war probably could not have been won without French aid. The French were, like the English, a major trading partner. Further, the French had fought their own revolution against their tyrannous rulers in 1789 and after, and Americans felt a good deal of sympathy for the French ideal of "liberty, equality, and fraternity." But under Napoleon, who had taken over during the governmental chaos that followed the revolution, France had proven to be an untrustworthy friend.

By the late 1790s, Americans were bitterly

James Madison was eager to keep America out of the continuing battle between the French and English, during which the combatants kept trampling on American rights. Remaining neutral proved to be difficult.

divided between those who favored England and those who favored France. At various times there came calls for war with England, war with France, or war with both. With Americans unable to agree what side they were on, it is hardly surprising that relations with both nations were very complicated indeed.

As the war between those two mighty nations dragged on, both began to trample on the rights of neutral nations, particularly those of the United States. They were like two angry boys fighting, who don't care if they are smashing up the furniture in the living room. For one thing, each insisted that Americans should not help the other one, which meant basically not to sell anything useful in wartime to either side. This included the things Americans most wanted to sell, like cotton, corn, fish, meat, timber. At various times, both countries instituted rules telling Americans what they could export and where they could ship their products. When Americans tried to ignore these rules, both British and French captured American merchant ships and seized the cargoes they were carrying. Year after year, Americans lost hundreds of ships and many millions of dollars in goods.

However, it was the English, with their powerful navy, who could best enforce their shipping rules on Americans. Sometimes they stationed their ships just outside American ports, where they could stop American ships if they suspected they were headed for French ports.

Worse, the English made a regular practice of capturing American sailors and forcing them to work on their own ships. The life of a sailor in the British navy was not much better than slavery. The British sailors were given poor food, slept in hot, cramped quarters, and were whipped for breaking minor rules. Nobody wanted to serve in the British navy if he could help it, and the English had to literally kidnap their own young men off the streets for naval duty. These men deserted whenever they had the chance, often in American ports. Many of these deserters took jobs on American vessels, where treatment was much better.

This engraving, made in 1812, shows British seamen dragging a sailor from an American merchant ship. Impressment of sailors from American ships was one reason why many Americans wanted to go to war with the British.

The British claimed the right to stop American ships and search them for such deserters. However, along with the British deserters they often found, they took helpless native-born American sailors to fill up their shortages of seamen and "impressed" them into the British navy. Over the years, some ten thousand Americans were impressed in this way.

All of these problems—the various embargoes against American shipping by the French and English, the seizure of millions of dollars in shipping and goods, the impressing of American sailors—stirred up a great deal of anger in American hearts.

Like President John Adams, Thomas Jefferson, president from 1801 to 1809, and James Madison, the next president, were determined to avoid war. They knew that the young nation could not afford to get itself involved in a bloody and expensive conflict with either of these powerful nations, much less both. Again and again they tried to smooth things over.

The first crisis came in 1807. That spring a number of deserting British sailors turned up in Chesapeake Bay. The local authorities offered them protection. Some of them even joined the American navy. One of these deserters, "a short, swarthy former tailor from London" named Jenkin Ratford, joined the crew of the U.S.S. *Chesapeake*. Unfortunately,

A cartoon showing how the embargo against shipping goods to the French and English was working—"Ograbme" is embargo spelled backward. In fact, the embargo proved an unworkable policy hurtful to New England commerce and was soon scrapped.

he took to jeering British officers he saw in the streets in Norfolk, where his ship was tied up.

When the *Chesapeake* put to sea, a British warship called the *Leopard* stopped it. The commander of the British ship was under orders to search the *Chesapeake* for deserters. The Americans would not let the British officer who came on board take anybody off. So the *Leopard* fired a shot across the bow of the *Chesapeake,* and when that did no good, fired into the ship itself, shelling it with several cannonballs. Three Americans were killed, and twenty were wounded. The captain of the *Chesapeake* was forced to surrender. The British then dragged off the helpless Ratford, as well as three other sailors who were American citizens.

The *Chesapeake* affair raised American anger to the boiling point. Once again there were cries for war. President Jefferson, however, was still determined to avoid war, and he got Congress to put through an embargo act, which stopped all foreign trade of any kind except along the coast from one American port to another. Within a short time it was clear that this rule was hurting American growers of corn and cotton, merchants, sea captains and their sailors more than it was hurting the English and the French. The law was modified to stop trade only with the English and French. This was ineffective, and so the law was modified once again. Still, nothing worked.

Meanwhile, on the western frontier of the nation something else was happening that also was raising tempers against the British. At bottom were problems with the Indians. All through the years leading up to the War of 1812, white settlers had continued to press into Indian lands. Again and again Indians were forced to make bad deals with white land speculators and various governmental authorities, trading away huge tracts of land for small amounts of money or goods. Finally, some Indians recognized that they must make a united stand against the whites. The most important of these were twins, the famous Tecumseh and his brother, who was known as the Prophet. Tecumseh in particular

The Shawnee leader known as the Prophet was the twin brother of the more famous Tecumseh. The two brothers tried to get the Indians on the frontier to give up alcohol and work together to defeat the whites.

began rallying the Indians, urging them not to drink the white man's whiskey, which in many cases had demoralized whole Indian villages. He asked them to join together in dealing with whites instead of trading away their land piecemeal.

Meanwhile, the borderlands in the area of what are now the states of Indiana and Illinois, saw scenes of constant skirmishing between Indians and whites, with men, women, and children being slaughtered on both sides. Many Americans on the western frontier believed that the British were stirring up the Indians against them and were supplying them with guns and ammunition. How much truth there is to this accusation is difficult to know. The British held Canada and maintained some forts around the Great Lakes, which they were supposed to have given up long

Many Americans believed that the British were paying the Indians to massacre them on the frontiers. There is no good evidence that this was true, but the belief helped to fuel American anger against England.

before as part of the peace treaty ending the Revolution over twenty years earlier. They continued to trade with the Indians, and they certainly wanted to maintain friendly relations with them. Whether they were actually encouraging the Indians to kill whole American families on their farms is another question.

In any case, the westerners on the borderlands demanded that something be done about the Indians. The man in charge was quite willing to take action. He was William Henry Harrison, governor of the Indiana Territory. In 1808 Tecumseh and his brother the Prophet had set up a large Indian village called Prophetstown on Tippecanoe Creek, in the center of what is now the state of Indiana. It was clear to Harrison that Tecumseh was hostile to whites and wanted them to advance no further into Indian territory. Harrison decided that war was inevitable and it

This cartoon manifests the belief of Americans that they could teach the English John Bull a lesson. In the middle the French Emperor Napoleon expresses hope that the United States will support him against England, while at right John Bull reads his lesson: power constitutes right.

would be best to strike first. He chose a moment when Tecumseh was away from Prophetstown, meeting with southern Indian groups. With a force of a thousand men, Harrison marched to Prophetstown and encamped just outside it for the night. In the town the Prophet worked his warriors up to a high pitch of excitement. Just about dawn they attacked, catching the sleeping Americans off guard. Harrison rallied his troops, forming them into a line. The Indians continued to battle back, firing at the Americans from behind trees, but the American force was too strong. The Indians were driven off, and the Americans destroyed their village.

Actually, the battle at Tippecanoe Creek was not in any way decisive. Tecumseh continued to organize the Indians, and they fought alongside the British in the coming war until Tecumseh himself was killed in the fighting. Moreover, the Americans suffered well over 250 dead and wounded, while the bodies of only thirty-eight Indians were found after the battle. Nonetheless, Americans considered it a great victory. Among other things, it made William Henry Harrison so famous that he was later elected president of the United States. This episode and the continuing fear of the Indians also deepened the hatred of Americans, particularly westerners, against the British, who were thought to be supplying the Indians.

Yet when you come down to it, neither the *Chesapeake* incident nor the Battle of Tippecanoe was important enough to fight a war over. The rights of neutrals on the high seas did matter and so did impressment, but British and French interference with American shipping did not really threaten American security or wealth in a truly serious way. So far as the Indian problems went, there was no good evidence that the British had anything to do with it.

It is true that some Americans hoped that a war with the English would give them an excuse to attack Canada and take it away from England, but most Americans were not ready to go to war for Canada.

The truth is that war could have been avoided in 1812, and once started, it could have been stopped much sooner than it was. Why, then, did so many Americans demand war in 1812?

The best answer we can give is that many, if not most, Americans were sick and tired of being pushed around by the British. It was the old story of the brave boy deciding he had to stand up to the neighborhood bully. This is what we mean when we say that the causes of the War of 1812 were at least partly psychological: the war came about as much because of how Americans felt about what was happening, as for any real danger to the country.

CHAPTER VI

The War Begins

Not all Americans, by any means, were eager for the fight. This was particularly true of the Federalists in New England. We remember that in the election of 1800 Americans had found themselves split into two factions, the Republicans and the Federalists. The Republicans tended to side with France, the Federalists with England; the Republicans believed that farmers were the backbone of America, the Federalists insisted that commerce was essential to American prosperity; the Republicans were strongest in the South and West, the Federalists in the North. Not surprisingly, then, New Englanders, especially the Federalists among them, wanted no part in a war against England. They sympathized with England against the French, and they wanted to go on doing business with British merchants. In time, these New England Federalists would cause much trouble for Madison in fighting the war.

But as we know the majority of Americans were fed up with England telling them who they could trade with and impressing their seamen, and in June 1812, the Congress declared war on England. Unfortunately, the Congress, while eager to fight, was not eager to spend money to do so.

American forces were weak and lacked a lot of necessary equipment. The navy consisted of a mere handful of ships to send out against the British fleet—the largest in the world. However, Americans thought they would be able to waltz through the British forces and take Canada away from the British. Unfortunately, the American generals in charge of the fighting there were incompetent and, in some cases, cowardly. The Americans were driven out of Canada, and by the time of the appointment of new

The Americans had far fewer warships than the British had, so the British had nearly free access to the American coastline. However, American seamen were generally better than the British. In this picture, painted from a drawing made on board the ship, the U.S. Frigate United States, *commanded by Stephen Decatur, one of the heroes of the War of 1812, has demasted the British Frigate* Macedonian.

generals who stiffened the spine of the army, the British had built up their own forces and the chance of taking Canada was lost.

The same ineptitude on the part of American officers was responsible for one of the greatest humiliations ever handed to the United States. American warships and their crews were as good as, or even better than, the British ones; but the British had far more ships than the Americans did. They were able to control American ports, keeping merchants' vessels bottled up at home. Worse, their sea power allowed them to land troops almost at will on American shores. Towns and villages up and down the Atlantic Coast, especially in New England, were often subjected to sudden forays by British troops, who would make off with whatever they could lay their hands on.

The worst of these inland forays came in August 1814. For some time the government in Washington had been worried that the British might try to attack the nation's capital. After all, there was a water route through Chesapeake Bay and up the Potomac practically to the doorstep of the White House. But, as ever, due to bungling by generals, no defenses were organized for the city. Then in mid-July a squadron of British ships sailed into the Chesapeake, and in August they landed some four thousand troops. The soldiers marched toward Washington with little opposition.

The capital was swept with rumors, and on August 22 residents began to flee the city in carriages and carts, taking with them whatever they could carry. In the White House, the President's wife, Dolly Madison, began to pack up her china and silverware. President Madison was out trying to make sense of the confusion, but the next day he realized that Washington was defenseless. He packed up what important papers he could, and he, too, left. On August 24, the British marched into the city. When their troops reached the White House, they found a meal for forty people cooked and ready to eat. The British admiral took a cocked hat of the President's and a cushion from Dolly Madison's

Dolly Madison, the popular wife of President James Madison, was forced by the British to flee the White House, taking with her as much as she could hastily pack.

favorite chair as souvenirs. They burned the White House and the Capitol, as well as other government buildings. They then made a leisurely retreat to their ships.

The British now sailed on up the Chesapeake to Baltimore. There they were stopped. At the mouth of Baltimore's harbor was Fort McHenry. The gunners from the British fleet and those in the fort bombarded each other, but the Americans proved to be the better gunners and the British

The British attack on Washington was a great humiliation for the United States and President Madison. In this cartoon "Maddy" is shown fleeing with state papers under his arm while spectators jeer.

fleet had to back off. The victory at Baltimore was some solace to Americans after the humiliation at Washington, but not much.

One other thing came out of the fight at Baltimore. During the night of the battle, a young lawyer had gone out to one of the British warships to arrange for the release of a friend who had been captured. He could not get back to land during the bombardment. All during the long night he stood staring into the darkness to see if the American flag still flew over Fort McHenry. At dawn he saw that it was still there. So excited was he that he began scribbling down a poem dedicated to the moment. The young lawyer was named Francis Scott Key, and the poem he wrote began with the lines, "Oh, say can you see, by the dawn's early light . . . ." Very soon the poem was published, and Key adapted it to the tune of a British ditty called "Anacreon in Heaven." Americans began singing it right away, although "The Star Spangled Banner" was not made the official national anthem until 1931. (You can see the actual flag that inspired the poem at the Smithsonian Institution in Washington.)

Given the ineptitude of American generals, it is a wonder that the British did not win the war. It was the American navy that saved the day. Although the British had far more warships than the Americans did, the American guns and their gunners were superior to the British ones. That was made clear on August 19, 1812, only a few weeks after Congress declared war, when the British frigate *Guerrière* came up against the American frigate *Constitution*. The British ship began banging away at the *Constitution,* but the American ship held fire and closed in until it was only a pistol shot away from the enemy. Then it unleashed a murderous cannonade. Very quickly it blew down the *Guerrière's* masts and killed and wounded many of the crew. Within half an hour the *Guerrière* was a worthless hulk. In the course of the battle, so many British cannonballs bounced off the *Constitution's* hull that the sailors started calling her "Old Ironsides."

Perhaps more significant were the naval battles on the Great Lakes. One of the first of these came in 1813, when Captain Oliver Hazard Perry, with some newly built ships, took on the British Great Lakes fleet. Once again through excellent American gunnery, Perry destroyed the British fleet. He wrote to his chief the now-famous line "We have met the enemy, and they are ours." Other American naval successes on the Great Lakes gave control of those waters to the Americans. While the United States was not able to take Canada, American naval superiority in the

Oliver Hazard Perry, shown here in an etching done from a painting. Perry was one of the expert American seaman who gave Americans something to cheer about in the War of 1812.

area ensured that the British could not mount an attack on the United States from that direction.

From all of this, it will be clear that the war was dragging on inconclusively. The British had burned parts of Washington and made forays into other villages and towns along the coast but had not been able to inflict any real damage on America. On the other hand, the Americans had not been able to defeat the British in any significant way, either. By 1814 a lot of Americans were tired of the whole thing and were looking for a way out. This was particularly true of the New England Federalists, who had opposed the war from the start. Moreover, the British, in hopes of keeping the New Englanders unenthusiastic about the war, were permitting ships to come and go from New England ports while not allowing shipping to ports farther south, like New York or Philadelphia. The result was that many New England merchants were actually supplying food and other supplies to the British even as the war was going on. Federalists in New England were looking for a way out of the war.

In the fall of 1814 a meeting of New England Federalists hostile to the war was held at Hartford, Connecticut. A few of the more radical dissidents hoped to pass resolutions calling for separation from the Union and a separate peace, but more moderate people were in the majority and the resolutions that were passed called merely for amendments to the Constitution. Nonetheless, the Hartford Convention made it clear that support for the war was eroding.

This cartoon of the Hartford Convention shows Rhode Island, Connecticut, and Massachusetts considering the possibilities of splitting from the Union and jumping into the arms of the British. In the end, they did not jump.

In fact, both sides had been trying to make peace almost from the moment the War of 1812 had started. Both James Madison and British officials at various times suggested terms for a peaceful settlement of the issues. Nothing came of these efforts. A beginning toward peace was made in 1812, only a few months after the war started, when a Russian official offered to mediate the conflict. The British turned the idea down, but in time it led the British to offer to negotiate directly with the Americans, and in 1814 these talks began at Ghent, Belgium.

By this time a lot had changed. The French had been beaten and Napoleon had resigned and had been exiled. European nations were holding a great meeting in Vienna to discuss changes to Europe as a result of the peace; to the English, the American war was a sideshow. With the European war over, neither the British nor the French were interested in interfering with neutral shipping.

The British-American talks went on for almost all of 1814, with each side making demands and jockeying for position. But both sides wanted to get out of the war, and in the end a deal was struck: everything would go back to the way it had been before the war, with the loose ends to be tied up at later meetings. So the war was finally over.

In reality, it was a war that nobody had won. The British had not given up what they claimed was their right to impress American seamen but, in fact, with the European war over, impressment was no longer an important issue.

But Americans did believe that they had won, if not the war, at least their self-respect. They had stood up to the bully and made him back down; and that seemed, to most Americans, something worth fighting for.

Ironically, one of the most famous battles of the War of 1812 was fought after it was over. With the war with the French over and Napoleon exiled to the island of Elba, the British could now concentrate their military strength on the United States. In 1815 they sent fifty ships carrying 7,500 troops under Sir Edward Packenham, one of England's leading commanders, to the Gulf of Mexico. Packenham's plan was to conquer New Orleans. With the city in his hands he could control the Mississippi, that critically important water route for Americans in the western land.

New Orleans was thinly defended, but fortunately for the Americans, General Andrew Jackson, commander of the American army in the Southwest, was able to hurry to the defense of the city with around 16,000 troops, mainly from Tennessee, Kentucky, and Louisiana. Packenham, instead of sailing up the Mississippi as everybody expected,

The Battle of New Orleans, a great victory for the United States, ironically was fought after terms of peace had been agreed. This picture shows the British troops under fire. In the foreground General Edward Packenham sits mortally wounded.

came in from the east via Lake Borgne. Jackson hastily brought his soldiers out to that side of the Mississippi, where they labored mightily to throw up a dirt and mud bastion. At one end of the bastion was the Mississippi, at the other a cypress swamp. Jackson skillfully arranged his cannons around and behind the bastion to cover the open ground in front of him.

When General Packenham arrived with his troops, he realized that he could not outflank the bastion, but would have to attack it directly. He tried, but American cannon fire on the unprotected British troops cut their lines to pieces. In less than half an hour the British had lost over 12,000 soldiers. Packenham himself was killed. The battle was over, and the British crept back to their ships and sailed away. Only thirteen Americans were killed. Sadly, this loss of life was unnecessary: the peace treaty had been signed two weeks before, but the news had not yet crossed the Atlantic.

The main effect of the War of 1812 on the United States was an uprush of patriotic feeling. Virginians, New Englanders, New Yorkers were coming to think of themselves as citizens of the United States more than they ever had. They took pride in themselves for having at least fought off the British bully and henceforth would insist on being seen as a truly independent power, able to stand up to anybody.

This attitude was heightened, not long after the peace treaty, with the victory over the Barbary pirates. For a long time previously, some of the nations along the North Africa coast, particularly Morocco, Algiers, Tripoli, and Tunis, had preyed upon European and American merchant shipping passing along their shores. Europeans had been making annual payments to the rulers of these nations to stop them from attacking their shipping, and after the United States became independent in 1783, it too, had made these payments. Jefferson decided to fight back. At first, American naval forces had few successes. In 1803 a warship named the *Philadelphia* ran aground in the harbor of Tripoli. The Tripolitans refloat-

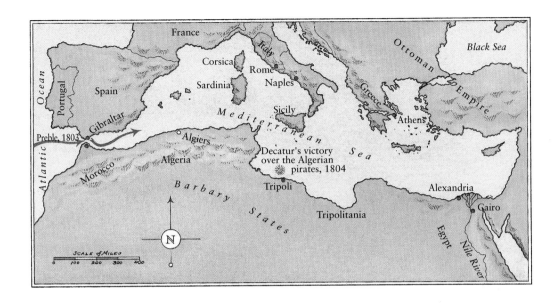

ed it and anchored it under the guns of their harbor fort to taunt the Americans. A few months later a young naval officer, Lt. Stephen Decatur, led a small detachment that recaptured the *Philadelphia*. In one battle, Decatur leaped onto an enemy ship carrying a cutlass and a pistol. The enemy captain knocked Decatur down, but Decatur shot him dead. In 1805 Tripoli gave up the fight and stopped harassing American shipping.

But other North African nations continued to make their attacks. As soon as the War of 1812 was over, Decatur, now risen to the rank of commodore, headed for Algiers with a large fleet. He rapidly took the enemy flagship and dictated terms to Algeria. Victories over the Barbary pirates increased Americans' sense of confidence and pride in their nation.

This attitude showed itself most especially a few years later when, in 1823, President James Monroe laid down the principle that no European power should attempt to establish more colonies in the New World. This mattered, because at the time many Latin American states were in rebellion against their European masters, especially Spain. European nations were trying to bring these breakaway colonies back under their

(above) The bombardment of
Tripoli by American ships
eventually forced the North
African nations to stop prey-
ing on American merchant
ships. Many Americans had
been captured and enslaved
by the Barbary pirates.

(right) Naval hero Stephen
Decatur not only gained
important victories in the
War of 1812 but conquered
Tripoli and ended the depre-
dations of the Barbary
Pirates on American ship-
ping.

control. Even Russia was establishing military posts on the Pacific coast in what is now northern California.

In fact the United States did not have the power to enforce the so-called Monroe Doctrine. The European powers simply did not take it seriously, and nothing much was done with it. But over time, as American power grew, the Monroe Doctrine became an important basis for American policy in the Western Hemisphere.

This period of American history, running from the election of Thomas Jefferson in 1800, into the 1820s, was very important for the way in which America consolidated itself into a true nation. At the beginning of the period, the United States was a collection of independent-minded states, who for only twelve years had been collected under a single roof. The acquisition of the huge Louisiana Territory had, in one stroke, opened the eyes of Americans to what a great nation the United States might be, if it could settle all the new lands it now owned. The decisions of the John Marshall Supreme Court step-by-step centralized power in the hands of the national government at the expense of the state governments. And the War of 1812 helped Americans to think of themselves as a single nation, quite prepared to challenge the powers of the mighty nations of Europe. Americans now felt that their nation belonged on the main stage with star actors.

BIBLIOGRAPHY

For Students

Blumberg, Rhoda. *The Incredible Journey of Lewis and Clark.* New York: Lothrop, Lee & Shepard, 1987.

Bober, Natalie. *Thomas Jefferson: Man on a Mountain.* New York: Atheneum, 1988.

Carter, Alden. *The War of 1812: Second Fight for Independence.* New York: Franklin Watts, 1992.

Cwiklik, Robert. *Tecumseh, Shawnee Rebel.* New York: Chelsea House, 1993.

Freedman, Russell. *An Indian Winter: Paintings and Drawings by Karl Bodmer.* New York: Holiday House, 1992.

Fritz, Jean. *The Great Little Madison.* New York: G.P. Putnam, 1989.

Marrin, Albert. *1812: The War Nobody Won.* New York: Atheneum, 1985.

Meltzer, Milton. *Thomas Jefferson: The Revolutionary Aristocrat.* New York: Franklin Watts, 1991.

Roop, Peter and Connie, eds. *Off the Map: The Journals of Lewis and Clark.* New York: Walker & Co., 1995.

Wexler, Sanford, ed. *Westward Expansion: An Eyewitness History.* New York: Facts on File, 1991.

For Teachers

Ambrose, Stephen E. *Undaunted Courage: Meriwether Lewis, Thomas Jefferson and the Opening of the American West.* New York: Simon & Schuster, 1996.

Appleby, Joyce. *Capitalism and a New Social Order: The Republican Vision of the 1790s.* Cambridge: Harvard University Press, 1994.

Banning, Lance. *The Jeffersonian Persuasion: Evolution of a Party Ideology.* Ithaca: Cornell University Press, 1978.

Ellis, Joseph. *American Sphinx: The Character of Thomas Jefferson.* New York: Knopf, 1997.

Freeman, Douglas S. *George Washington: Vol. 6, Patriot and President.* New York: Scribner, 1953.

McCoy, Drew R. *The Elusive Republic: Political Economy in Jeffersonian America.* Chapel Hill: University of North Carolina Press, 1980.

Malone, Dumas. *Jefferson the President: First Term, 1801–1805.* Boston: Little Brown, 1970.

Page numbers for illustrations are in **boldface**.

trade, 12, **16**. *See also* commerce;
    fur trade
    embargoes, 61–62, **63**, 64
    with England during War of 1812,
        76–77
    Indians with English, 24, 35
    right of deposit, 25–26
transportation
    and hostilities between British and
French, 61
    of products, 12, 25–26
    regulation of, 56
    shipping, 12, **16**
    steamboat, 54–56, 55
trappers, 24. See also fur trade
Trenton, NJ, 54
Treasury Department, 20
Tripoli, 80–81, **82**
Twelfth Amendment, 17

United States, **71**

vice president, electing, 15–16

voters, leaders' views of, 13

War Department, 20
War of 1812, 11
    causes of American involvement,
        59–69
    military preparedness for, **71**, 71–72
    naval battles, **71**, 75–76
    outcome of, 78
    and patriotic feeling, 80
Washington Territory, 10
Washington, George
    and banking, 51–52
    opinion of voters' judgment, 13
    Presidential election of, 9, 11
    and scope of government, 11–13
Washington D.C.
    British attack on, 72–73, **74**
    early days as capital city, 20
Wm. Cutting, 55

Yazoo case, 47–48
yellow fever, 25–26

JAMES LINCOLN COLLIER is the author of a number of books both for adults and for young people, including the social history *The Rise of Selfishness in America*. He is also noted for his biographies and historical studies in the field of jazz. Together with his brother, Christopher Collier, he has written a series of award-winning historical novels for children widely used in schools, including the Newbery Honor classic, *My Brother Sam Is Dead*. A graduate of Hamilton College, he lives with his wife in New York City.

CHRISTOPHER COLLIER grew up in Fairfield County, Connecticut and attended public schools there. He graduated from Clark University in Worcester, Massachusetts and earned M.A. and Ph.D. degrees at Columbia University in New York City. After service in the Army and teaching in secondary schools for several years, Mr. Collier began teaching college in 1961. He is now Professor of History at the University of Connecticut and Connecticut State Historian. Mr. Collier has published many scholarly and popular books and articles about Connecticut and American history. With his brother, James, he is the author of nine historical novels for young adults, the best known of which is *My Brother Sam Is Dead*. He lives with his wife Bonnie, a librarian, in Orange, Connecticut.

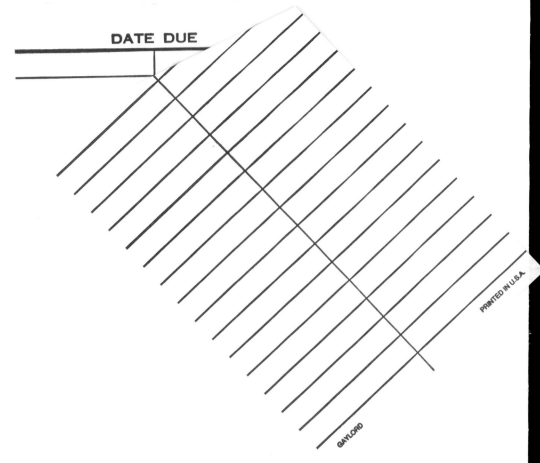

DATE DUE

GAYLORD

PRINTED IN U.S.A.